THE WALL STREET GAME

GAME RECOGNIZE GAME

YUL SPENCER

IAM Enterprises

CONTENTS

DISCLAIMER

Neither IAM Enterprises, nor any of its directors, officers, shareholders, personnel, representatives, agents, or independent contractors (collectively, the "Operator Parties") are licensed financial advisers, registered investment advisers or registered broker-dealers. None of the Operator Parties are providing investment, financial, legal, or tax advice, and nothing on www.wallstsmarts.com (henceforth, "the Site") or in the Wall Street-Smart Series of books, should be construed as such by you. The books and the Site should be used as educational, informational and entertainment purposes only and are not replacement for professional investment advice.

THERE IS HIGH RISK IN TRADING!

The full disclaimer may be found at the end of this book.

JOIN THE THOUSANDAIRE MOVEMENT

Thousandaire members get unique items and are always the first to hear about Yul Spencer's new books, publications and public appearances.

See the back of the book for details on how to sign up.

"A lot of people are advocating that the rich get richer and the poor get poorer. Well, that's only because you don't understand, but it's gonna happen to you.

You see it's all just a game, ladies and gentlemen, and the quality of your living depends entirely on your ability to play the game.

And I play the game."

--The Game

When I sub-titled this book "Game Recognize Game" a phrase used by some street-smart folks, my editor asked me why it isn't plural? I explained to her it isn't how we say it on "main street." We didn't "recognizes" game. It's not meant to be plural. It's meant to be singular in purpose. I see you. I recognize what you're up to specifically. If it's Wall Street or a street hustler, the game is recognized because it's sh** you've done unto us since the beginning of time. We're not all rich, but we're rich in personality. And that's the game on "main street." If you have a rich personality, it can take you where you want to go for the most part. Hollywood, New York City, Miami, but it won't pay bills or set you up for retirement, playas and playettes.

On Wall Street, it's not personality that makes you rich, it's knowledge others don't have yet and the disregard for main street. And if you can play the game on Wall Street, you can pay your bills and have a retirement fund. And they know that, but you don't know that and that's how they want to keep it.

It's a shame, it really is, but once someone with "game" recognizes it is a game and you get to play it and get paid racks on racks. You could nip that whole not having an extra four hundred dollars for emergencies in the bud. Back in the day you had to jump through hoops to play the Wall Street game. Really. You had to jump out of your car, get a newspaper and payphone back then. Which made it difficult as hell to win. If you can play, why shouldn't you? The whole idea behind this book series is to encourage those who thought they couldn't play the game.

Wall Street has developed into a game because of the evolution of greedy people. They want it all and they don't care if main street partakes in getting paid from the wealth of this country that they live and die for. The consumer bought up all this sh** and guess who the professional consumers are? Main street - the other forty to fifty percent of America that don't take any money from the stock market. That's mind blowing, especially when so many of us need money. Up to now main street has been the losers in this game. Every game has losers and winners. It's what makes it a game. The billionaires have kept main street baffled by the entire thing and then they act like they have nothing to do with it. Psychology is a huge part of this game and they have the money to fu** with all of ours every day with the support of the news media outlets they own.

Wall Street is ruled by the trillion-dollar hedge funds, billionaires, millionaires and AI (artificial intelligence). MARKET MAKERS are what they're called. The ones that create the game and its rules. Eighty percent of the money in the market is in there because of these entities. The other twenty percent are fireman, teachers, police pension funds, retail investors and so on. You and me. Maybe not you, yet.

It's possible this book could be your first book ever about Wall Street that you were willing to read. If so, thank you. If not, and you decide to get in the Wall Street Game, you will be what they call a "retail investor" one of the twenty percent. Now none of these entities that make the market work consider or include those of us on main street. I know main street knows this because some of them have been protesting for years to no avail. The big money keeps finding ways to make the market work for them and not for the lesser of us. That's why it's now a game. Do the math - they're winning. The so-called one percent have most of the money in the world and the rest of us do not. I'd say they're kicking our ass if it were a sport. They take the money every day from an economy that we all bust our backs to contribute to.

The gap created between them and us continues to get bigger and if I can have anything to do with closing that gap even a little, I'd sleep sometimes. What if? We all got back at them and crowded the market with our "twos and fews" (with what money we all have) collectively it could throw the economies inequality off some. Let's say twenty-five percent of main street creates an extra income using the stock market. I think it would freak the rich out and increase the wealth of many hoods and of many populations, especially in those rural towns who have been left out of the game for so long.

They have and they continue to build high power tools today to keep their foots on the neck of main street. To confuse the average wage earner who has found a foot in investing or trading for a living. They use all of them to rid themselves of all the smaller accounts and the players who have them. Me and maybe you.

Now, because of progress, we (retail investors) also have tools that weren't available to any of us in the past. Not having high speed internet or laptops, iPad, or cellphones made us easier victims for the wealthy. But that's in the past. We now can get and know as much information to make a profitable decision in the stock market as they can. I don't think they saw that coming. Especially the real old players. We used to be prey, you might say, or "new meat." You don't want to ever be called "new meat" not in any tight surroundings, anyway.

These tools will allow the other forty to fifty percent of America to begin winning the game on their end. Yes, I'm suggesting that we all start becoming "gamers" and take this money from the rich people who put it out for the taking every day because they're sure you're too scared to take it from them. They feel good about themselves because they put it in front of all our faces every day and we for all these decades let it go right by us. Because they're good at giving main street the feelings, not the facts. They're always working the psychological angle. And they make sure main street feels excluded from the game. Tha's game, baby. They say here it is. Come take some of my billions and many Americans with mini-computers in their pockets don't check it out or aren't drawn in. Why? You need the money. Take it.

A stand-up comic always knows what to open with - a trader must know when to close.

None of us want to feel less than, but we do. I'm referring to how most of the ninety-nine percent are made to feel, not how they actually feel. I can't call it. We're mostly made (primed) to feel this way about our finances/money in this society. We don't feel less than all the time obviously, but most of the time because becoming millionaires and billionaires is a must in this country. And you won't be happy until you do it. Especially if you're invested in equities the stock market.

The stock market must mean riches. The only reason for someone to be in the stock market is to get rich, otherwise you're wasting your time. No one cares about getting anyone started investing who may only have let's say fifteen hundred dollars or less to invest with. And I mean to their name maybe their entire savings if they have one. Oh, no you're primed to spend it and be without it forever unless of course you go back to work to make more money to save it up just to spend it again and again and again considering you have a job to go to. Having more than enough money for you, your family, friends and causes (whatever amount that might be) for the rest of your lives is not something that's often promoted or suggested. Not really.

What if you only needed thousands of dollars and not millions or even billions to maintain a deserving lifestyle? What's wrong with that, I ask? More than enough ain't enough for most people. I think as a culture we need to rethink this getting rich in America thing. If you're not "ballin'," you ain't happening.

Let me share something with you. I can buy all the balls I want, now that I have the m-o-n-e-y, who needs more than a couple balls, anyway. No pun intended. I can buy pieces of a "ball" corporation and I'm a long way off from becoming a millionaire. I'm like 950,000.00 down, but I do have thousands of dollars now and that will buy a lot of balls so I could be "ballin'!" If I bought the right ball corporation's stock, I could keep the dream of becoming a millionaire alive and I'm making money as I go along for the ride waiting for this great ball corporation to become profitable. See, when you own a stock of a corporation and it makes money, you make money, a huge amount of the time. There are always exceptions. #Thieves

The point is, we must stick to our objectives. I cover that in my first book (Wall Street Smarts). Your objective must be vividly clear. Crystal! It's fifty percent of the Wall Street Game for the thousandaire. Never forget that it's fifty percent of what you need to know to become a CPT (consistently profitable trader). Always keep that in perspective. Live your risk, not anyone else's. Don't let yourself leave you without a cash balance ever.

Opportunity is always lurking around the corner just like on them real streets. We always got to have our heads up and enough cash on hand to swoop on those opportunities that present themselves. #FlashCrash

This is my third book and the most wonderful realization came to me since I wrote the first two. It's we're not in competition with anyone, anybody or any hedge fund on Wall Street or any other street except the ones we live on. It hit me like a brick realizing that there was no competition in sharing with ninety percent of Americans on the way to becoming a "thousandaire" or at minimum to have over four hundred extra dollars on hand.

No one cares about us. No other books are written specifically for us. Even the beginning trader books won't turn you onto the "game" of Wall Street. They treat you like you bring nothing to the table so you should start at the beginning.

I agree there's a lot to learn at the beginning of your investment lifestyle. I don't agree your beginning should start in a beginner's book. A lot of it is a waste of time, especially for anyone with "Wall Street Smarts." We hit 'em when no one's looking or cares to know you're even in the room. #WallStGame

Before we get started on our rip-roarin' ideas 'bout the stock market. I'd like to with all my heart and every bit of humility I can relate to each of you through these pages. You can imagine my emotions right now? While typing this, I look like actors do when they get Emmys. I want to say thank you to all of the "real" folk, my "main street" folk, my OG's that bought and got this book and its purpose. I hear it's being passed around the neighborhoods. #ThankYou

You're in the captain's chair now, so in this book I'm most interested in how much you all have learned since the first two books? (Wall Street Smarts and Turning Losers into Winners In The Stock Market) I know in my heart and after some simple analysis that millions of you could use the knowledge still and the money but how much of the information have you absorbed, applied and remembered? I hear many of you are making that extra $400.00 that so many Americans seem to be missing in their accounts. I love hearing that. #Emails

If we're anything alike and I like to think we are a lot alike no matter what your background is. We're all in the same lifeboats without an extra four hundred dollars to our names. Well, not anymore, but you get the point. We're out here in the sea of American living trying to deposit these racks on a regular (money). I always find myself going back and referring to the recipe I learned in whatever book I got it out of to make sure I missed nothing before I heat up the stove. So, that's what we'll do in this book go back and check our recipes and more (strategies).

I'm sincerely serious about everyone getting this information and becoming thousandaires. I will see to it no person is left behind any longer or going without an extra four hundred dollars in their purse or wallet if I can help to do anything 'bout it, 'bout it. I'm like $NKE, "JUST DO IT." I'm not asking for permission or if my family and friends think it's a good idea. I know I'm not the most brilliant "At-home fund manager" or writer out there but I believe so many others are more brilliant than I am and have a steady job and would be better at taking advantage of the markets than I have been but someone has to let 'em know it's okay to get in and that's me. I'm just the only one for now who gives a fu** and is willing to write books about the stock market before reaching a million or billionaire dollar fund. It's unnecessary to achieve a million-dollar fund when these thousands could help so many Americans come up now. #DontBeLeftBehind

I write these books for people who grew up like myself or something similar and didn't have the advantages of the Ivy League. It's time someone expressed at the top of his lungs (paper) how easy it is for them to take this money. You don't have to be Ivy League to do well in the stock markets like we all used to think. Shoot, you can be you.

I sure would love to trade that kind of money someday surely now that I know how to trade but it's unnecessary to be trading millions of dollars to share with folks like myself with a limited bankroll. Sh** you can't wait to get a million, well you can, but you shouldn't. That's all I'm saying. With managing money it's not always about making money, well it is, but it's more about having money at all times. More than enough money for your lifestyle, not Elon Musk's.

Managing your own money in the stock market keeps you liquid my peoples. It's how so many of the people you aspire and admire to be like, keep their money growing. They just have more of it to grow.

That should not stop you. Think about this for a minute if you're willing to do all these "gigs" that are offered into today's job market, ridesharing, food delivery, weed delivery and of course exotic dancing, etc. These are some hard-working folks that could compound interest and be earning dividends if they thought they could or should. I'm of the belief some of you have more Wall Street-Smarts than you're aware of and I want to encourage the masses not to overlook those skills just because others do. Trip on this fact. Most citizens of this great United States work their asses off. If you don't believe me, look at grandpa. Go ahead, real quick like... No ass! It's due to how hard we work each week. Most of us 40 to 60 hours a week. Some of us 80. Wouldn't it behoove you take some time out of a month to figure out how you're spending that money say an hour a month? You have all the tech these days to do it with. When I was growing up, we had to use payphones. Your phones are now "paying-phones" you can get paid with it using a myriad of payment methods. And you can invest with it too. Wow, what an exciting time to be alive. So now that you see what the possibilities are, let's explore this game - The Wall Street Game.

THUS FAR

IF YOU'VE READ my previous books, you probably have learned a few strategies by now and perfected a trading method that works for you. You've decided you're a day trader, swing trader, options, or long-term investor. My strategy has more to do with my objectives and being adaptive and a monster about risk management. That's it really. Buy low, sell high, do the opposite of what most participants do. We'll discuss more of that before the end of this book.

Now you know I always suggest Googling sh** - almost everything, which we will still do but this time I'll be more specific about what to google. A tight friend of mines told his kid after he approached him with homework that Google is smarter than he will ever be. I thought that was a helluva an honest thing to tell his son. I thought that's some parenting skills 101 right there. Because we know he's not lying to his needy son, right?

We'll discuss upgrading your trade station if you haven't already (Computers and Screens). I'll share with you what equipment I started out on and how my trading paid for the units I work on now in my office.

Have you learned how to read the stock charts and the candlesticks which I have found really helpful? Reading the sticks can really help you understand what's going on in the trade in real time.

If you're a new reader, what got me started writing these books is learning that ninety percent of Americans didn't have an extra 400.00 to their name. When Andrew Yang #MATH (Make America Think Again), ran for President, he promised he'd give every American a thousand-dollar dividend. You should see how many folks Googled the word "dividend" that day. Most of your neighbors, friends and family don't even know what a dividend is or what it would mean to their financial situation. I think you do by now. It's not something usually discussed at Da Club. It should be, but not usually. #LOL But the Stock Market passes out dividends all the time, all year, every year for the most part.

They just don't discuss it or promote it amongst the least of us. Those of us on main street, the real streets earning less than a 100k a year. You're worth more to them in a hospital than you are on the job. You must start thinking about your financial life in the long-term instead of this micro-wave thinking we've been conditioned to think. Like we need everything right now. Do we? Not really, but first you must start believing you're going to be here in the long term. #Health

So much of main street thinks short term because of what they see in the world and on them streets. I get you but you will probably live through it whatever it is and be here in the long term and if I'm right, you will need money. Nevertheless, those folks on Wall Street been getting paid dividends for like forever without us and we sit around tripping on why they stay rich and we're not. You know what's crazy? The average American separate from his job's 401k could get these dividends too. I try to contain myself when folks tell me they have a 401K from their job. I ask, "Oh you do? Can you withdraw 400.00 from it right now?" You know the answer, right? NO. So what good is that money if it's not available to you now. #RealTalk

Now don't get me wrong, some jobs make you do this and it's not a bad idea. Well, it kind of is. I'll tell you why because if your job as a company goes under, fails to exist, you will lose your money 401K right along with them. Just ask the employees of many of these huge companies that are no longer with us or just hanging on or making a comeback like $GE. Their lifetime shareholders are pissed you hear me.

If you have to have a 401k at your job to have the job, then by all means do it. It's not illegal for you to get your own personal fund #IRA to do your own business with and invest in as many corporations as you want, allowing your money to grow and remain liquid. Instead of being subjected to one holding, that happens to be your job. Mr. Yang didn't make it to the presidency, but he sure brought awareness to how Americans need a Universal Basic Income especially during these Covid-19 times. I doubt seriously that this country will ever let that happen. Tha's why they call it "free-dom," you're dumb if you think you're getting something for free. What I believe in is you the student of the game and the institution of trade that will go on forever at least for our lifetime. Don't you think it's best to start your own fund so you can have your own UBI?

Once the average American changes his perception about the market and his abilities to get the money out of it and about having to become a millionaire or billionaire to be in the market in first place, I think you will see some real economic change for most Americans.

. . .

If you know my first two books, I'm only interested in the making of thousandaires all around the country. I hope many Americans have realized from reading those books that it's not a bad thing to have grands instead of millions. If you're reading this book, I'd like to believe you have changed the idea that "everybody" can become millionaires (Kardashians) and are happy knowing you can be a thousandaire and happy if not happier than many millionaires. Becoming a thousandaire is something you can accomplish without the pains of millions of dollars. Having an extra 40K in the "spur of the moment" can be very fulfilling for a person who has lived broke most his or her life an extra 10k or more for anything you want can make you feel like millions without the millionaire's burden. My goal for Americans is not only doable but believable. So, have you learned about dividends and how to find the companies that pay the highest yields and what that means for a company that can pay dividends and where they get the money to pay 'em? If you have, then you already are doing pretty good at turning a lil' money into a lot. #Alchemist

TELEVISION

THE TV SHOW "MAD MONEY" (you can get on the phone too #lol) is like the only show who helps the average TV watcher with cable and who is off of work every day by 3pm. Thank goodness for the internet that you can replay Jim Cramer's vids when you get home from work if you want. He keeps his audience up on things for the most part. Some of his picks are expensive or overvalued, but nobody is perfect at this. Obviously, he needs a hand getting the word out though he's been doing the show for over thirteen years. And the stats still say less than half of Americans believe they can earn money in the stock market. Yeah, homie could use a hand and so could these other shows and publications because none of them have you, the 99% in mind. Those shows aren't for us. Wink, wink. You should watch 'em, tho. Most of the shows are underlining conservative views (learn to overlook unless you agree of course) and I do mean politically conservative, so they're not cool to watch for the ninety-nine percent (inclusive groups). They give off the vapors that the show isn't for you. They guide only a certain part of America. They're not well diversified in staffing you might say or audience participants. So, the result is most Americans go without the greatest vehicle in the world to accumulate wealth in their lives today, right now, first thing tomorrow. #Easy

To be fair, I gotta give Mr. Cramer props. He does the best he can for the viewers that watch his show. So as you get more educated about the stock market and your objectives, check out "Mad Money" and see how if any of your objectives will fit with what Cramer is talking about that day. If nothing else, you'll be a little wiser by watching this insider help as many outsiders as he can. Even the youth. Yeah, he helps parents talk to their kids about the stock market. I was watching him the other day, and he said the schools are quick to teach kids how to slip a condom on a banana but not financial well-being. I thought that was funny, and it drove home an excellent point. It's up to us to teach ourselves and our kids. #WallStreetSmarts

Homie likes to quote Maya Angelou a lot. I think it's his way of telling the audience he's culturally diversified. The thing is, so many of us in these "real" streets have never read Maya Angelou. We're not even as culturally diversified as he is. #LOL

No one on Wall Street will make an admission to this fact that they keep this important information from you because they do it all in plain view. So, it couldn't be their fault that main street isn't attracted to what they're selling but thank goodness for you. I'm not on Wall Street and you're probably not either. I'm on Burbank Blvd and you're probably on 47th St in some major city or out in the country living off of a Frontage Road. So, have as much concern for them as they have for you and learn to "take the money." If I had a show, we'd call it "Funny Money" cuz I'm funny get it? "You'll run outta money before I run outta funny."

. . .

Other shows to watch are on Bloomberg, Yahoo and Cheddar. Cheddar is set up with a millennial vibe. You can find all kinds of lil' shows by every kind of trader out there on YouTube. Most can be useful. Others are a waste of time, but that will be up to you to decide how you value your time and who you resonate with. I listen to mostly everybody, but I particularly enjoy listening to contrary opinions - the other side you might say.

There are sentiment indexes and sentiment charts and meters, but I like to hear from as many partici-pants as I can listen to. I read everything too. For me it's a better gauge to hear from people even if they're lying or making sh** up. For some reason I can tell, and I think many of you can too. It's intuition, it's instinctual. It's what I like to call Wall Street Game but instead of getting pissed-off about the games they play, we take the money (sidenote: I was in that movie *Two Can Play That Game*). Anger doesn't pay well, anyway. Insiders and outsiders are worth listening to but please just listen. Don't react. Wait and check what they say out for yourselves. #DueDiligence

·   ·   ·

It's like most of the "systems" in our beautiful American culture. They seemed to have been created only for those with more or those who are expected to earn and inherit more. The only system created with the least in mind is the prison system. So, it's up to us to learn the value of these institutions and benefit from what we learn because they don't give a rat's ass about us. See, if you think about it, it isn't Wall Street that's the problem. We need a market; we've always had a market and always will have a market. It's necessary or you wouldn't be eaten food tonight.

This culture was cultivated on Wall Street by those who now fill the office buildings of these trillion-dollar hedge funds. They've become assholes for the most part. There are some who are genuinely great human beings, but they are too far and few for the American people to benefit from. So, we have what we have. But if this book gets any legs at all and we can form a main street gang of investors that get more involved in their financial futures and well-being (health) we can tip the scales or at most gain the extra money needed for our families and ourselves instead of waiting, waiting, and more waiting. For what? Who knows, but we do a lot of it. While in plain view every day, there's a consistent opportunity that exist right in front of our faces now. Not down the road but now.

So, I'm like I better let the homies know about it and create some real awareness that there's a real opportunity to take money for themselves legally from a developing economy that you helped develop. #GitUrMoney

We can do this by starting with getting our "money up" in the stock market. Why shouldn't you benefit from your self-learning? I remember the day I got serious about investing as a business. One day I heard my inner-being-self whatever you like to call it tell me... You like money so much why don't you learn about it? I talked back to myself and said that sounds like a good idea. Simple, I know, but my quest began that day. I'm not sure if my inner being said you like money so much or did it say, you need money so much why don't you learn about it? My heart says I got into this purely out of the need to have more money in my daily life. To maintain and manage the money I was already earning instead of becoming a professional consumer. Spend, spend, spend you can't win. You have to. You must learn to invest and make more money. And that's the money you can spend on whatever you say, but you never lose your principal if your risk management skills are tight. Never invest what you can't lose. #Rules

When you begin to diligently study a few of these shows and all the books you will read, you'll find out you can get up to speed with the markets rather quickly. You will catch up on these half-truths, characterization of words, headlines full of general semantics (alternative facts... they're lies in the hood). #FOS

I get it. You're probably maybe thinking why he would suggest we watch this crap? Well, because it isn't all crap. I got that word from the north. Well the reason is for only one reason and it's because everyone else does, especially when they tell you they don't or they're not. You begin to and I would suggest this listen to all of it with a sense of humor. Wear it like a loose garment. Joke with it. Know you're probably not getting the full story and dissect it for yourself and use only what you can use. Like a sponge. Use what you need and squeeze out the excess. And when it gets repetitive and bombastic mute the sh**! Or turn it off completely for a while. Believe me you'll feel soothed and better.

What we're listening for is the overall sentiment and where we are in the markets cycle and how's everyone feeling and acting. It helps me determine some of the Invisible intangibles and whispers in the market. Now, I wouldn't say this was a fact but when the folks on television in particular the Caucasian ones are smiling and sh** acting all happy especially when the market is supposedly "tanking" (semantics), it's a sign that the liquidity in the market is just fine and we're still rolling forward. And when they're not all happy and sh** the opposite has occurred credit has dried up companies like usual are highly overvalued and they start reporting like the Armageddon is coming so the reaction from the people who watch these shows is SELL, SELL, SELL, and that's when our opportunity to get in and win and win big shows up.

· · ·

How's that happen, you say? Fear. Greed plays a role too, but people with the greed and fear react emotionally. They hate to suffer any losses, so they bail out suffering much loss. In most cases, if they could've stayed in, they would've made their money back and more, but the market has a lot of leverage in it. People who borrow money to trade. So, if the markets start bottoming out, they have to get out and that can inflict serious losses on their funds. This might surprise you but when you realize that there are human beings (I like to think of them as human doings not beings) behind every trade you'll come to believe that Mrs./Mr. Market doesn't give a flyin' fu** that they borrowed money to trade. He doesn't, she doesn't care about feelings. It has no problem falling way down for a day or two or even years in the past, but eventually what it does and seem to care about is it keeps going up. It's only direction. But then it would be too late for those who get calls to pay what they owe. These are some terrible stories we small players hear about often and they scare us, but they don't affect us at all because we don't have margin calls to answer. After a while sure the market may get down here and there. Sometimes way down (crash) but it always gets back up and moves higher.

Please take some time to read about the history of Wall Street, who we don't really hate, we just didn't know. #RealTalk

Read about it. You'll see they're not as smart as they come off to be and they're certainly not necessarily but in some cases smarter than you and me. Another thing I like (in everything I look for things I like) about the TV shows is the ticker tape that scrolls the prices into view. I like it. I don't know why, but I like the scroll. It mesmerizes me. Maybe hypnotizes me but I'm able to monitor prices at an instant and I like that. Obviously, I'm attracted to the bright lights. #Actorslife

PERCEPTIONS

IN MY FIRST BOOK, *Wall Street Smarts*, I suggested you Google, "general semantics" and study all about it. Have you? Well, here's me reminding you. It's how the idea of a third book came about to connect with you again and clarify or reignite an idea you might've forgotten about by now. It's a difficult task to write in one or two books all the different dynamics that we come upon daily, weekly, or monthly in the stock market as investors. "The Invisibles" is what I call those intangibles. We can't or don't know or don't see but that shouldn't hinder us from making money once we understand their existence in the market.

· · ·

However, I have to constantly remind myself of what I'm doing in the market, beginning with knowing my clear objectives. Again, yes, I know. Objectives, objectives.

I want everybody to know and gather the confidence that they can get this money legally and without filling out a bunch of paperwork! I betcha didn't know that. It surprises me how many Americans don't know how simple it is to open an account and begin investing into themselves. It boggles my mind, really.

We don't like a lot of paperwork, do we? That is another psychological game that has been hindered by the internet. Shoot, most folks from where I'm from got tired of all the paperwork that makes you feel like you're not getting the job, loan or home anyway. You think they needed all that paperwork? No. It was a set-up to discourage folk with less patience for authority or authority figures like the loan officer, police officer or your probation officer. We don't like 'em and those in power knew that and used it to keep us out the game. So, these days it takes virtually no paperwork to open an account and get into business for yourself buying pieces of corporations. That's amazing, that's America. I find it important to clarify this to the Americans who didn't know that. If I didn't know any better, you'd think I was revealing some secret, but it isn't. It's just a secret to main street or simply ignored by them entirely. Main street's perception in general of the market is if you ask almost any of them is that it's gambling, it's corporate greed, it's only for rich folk. That's not true at all.

I'm sure we all know by now (maturity) bad sh** happens in every industry. Wall Street is no different. You've seen the movies and news specials. Let me tell ya' millions of people come to my town (Hollywood, CA) every year gambling that they're the next hot thing in music, acting, or whatever. Hollywood breeds gamblers and what we gamble with is ourselves with a high probability that you won't make it. And even if you do, if you don't know money you will give it back in probate, restitution, or some funky lawsuit. This town gives nothing without a plan to get it back. It's just business. #Royalties

. . .

We're the commodity and if you're not "hot" your talent won't matter. I hope some of my colleagues get this book so they could put a financial foundation under their fragile career choices. And what about after the career is over and you're old or you don't feel like doing it anymore or when a slowdown hits your career? What if you get disabled? What if you already are? (My daughter is the first female wheelchair actor to hit Sundance and Cannes in 2019). I'm just saying, I'm speaking from experience. Knowing how to get this money sitting on your ass could become helpful if you knew how to get it. We don't know what we don't know. #Hollywood

The point is as I've mentioned earlier, we're all aware of the bad sh** that happens to millions of people in this industry (showbiz) you watch the shows and tabloids. You know the dangers but if I asked you, hold up, not me but IF, Steven Spielberg called you right now and interrupted your reading and asked you to be in a movie tomorrow you'd probably be flattered and probably say yes. #HighestProbability

. . .

You would say that was good news knowing that it could turn all bad that you could also become the next sad story of Hollywood. But most of us would do it anyway. I don't know a business or an industry without some rotten apples in it. You can reject anything you don't know anything about but once you know, then you know and then you can do. So, it's these kinds of perceptions that the stock market is only for the well-to-do, it's too risky for the average person or you're not smart enough are some of the reasons that keep hard-working folk from ever having more than enough MONEY! #FIRE

I'm hoping these books could help put an end to those kinds of perceptions and beliefs by getting billions of you to see you're smart enough to get these thousands or millions if that's what you want. If you follow your own rules, you'll minimize any risks that are out there like we do with the rest of our lives. #Undefeated

Have the confidence in you to know now that these markets and money taking are not only for the well-to-do but it's for you too.

THE JOURNAL

THE STOCK MARKET is a dynamic and mesmerizing event to a point that sometimes if we haven't written our rules down, we'll forget 'em. What you learn will go into one ear and when you nap will pour out the other. #Journal

So, your journal will be immensely useful to you. Here's where you write all your detectives notes and your rules for investing and trading. Taking notes from all those books you've read. I have many journals I use to track and hunt down mostly distressed stocks and their companies. I account for my capital and risk management. I write these things down. I suggest you don't leave it up to your computer to keep in track of you. #Olskool

Usually I find great companies with a bad balance sheet for now. It's why the stock is usually down and when they clean up their act the stock goes back up again. I do this type of hunting time and time again. It's routine now. And I "turn the loser stock into a winner" by waiting on it to get its act together. So really, I didn't do sh** but wait. The work that I did do was just that *wait*. It sounds easier than it is, but it's work believe me. To conquer oneself will be the biggest challenge one ever faces.

Even though it gets easier once you learn how to profit because of it. While waiting you begin looking for your next opportunity. Wash, rinse and repeat. I told you I was going to slip you some knowledge you could use by opening bell. I know it's too simple for the complicated alpha but don't let all that learning get you twisted. Don't you be so smart you do something stupid. Never be in a hurry to lose money. #WallStGame

. . .

We can only move on what we know and learn to do the due diligence on the companies we want to invest in. The folks on Wall Street don't know anything about your ideas or objectives for the future. And we don't have to fully understand anything about all their complicated ways of manipulating and maneuvering the market up and down to make our money. #Boom

If you can grasp this, you can stay paid up in these markets. However, if you allow the "noise" to move you in and out of your investments it won't go well for you, my friend. Now, I get my bright ideas from getting out of the house going shopping or just riding around town and seeing what's new in office buildings, franchises, and in what direction everyone's driving.

When it comes down to tracking stocks, the journal is a necessity some folks call this paper trading where you act like you bought a hundred shares of something and see what happens. I guess paper trading can be useful for traders with absolutely no time in the chair (in front of the screens). The tracking and hunting I'm writing about in my journal have to do with actual trades I want to take. Businesses I'm serious about putting money into. I've determined what my objectives are like I've asked you all to do and I write them down every day in my journal. I know what my risk threshold is and I write that down too so I don't all of a sudden change it in the middle of a buy. My risk amount is specific, and I stick to it and adapt along the way. When I started with only fifteen hundred dollars, I would only risk 200.00 on each investment or trade. Now I'm ready to ask my myself my favorite question. Who will make more money this year with my two hundred dollars? Me? Microsoft? CVS? Or so and so? Then I make a decision. You must learn how to make decisions rather quickly or you will miss your moment of entry or exit.

It becomes easier to invest in this extraordinary economy once you've learned how to trade. It's like stocking your own ATM. However, after asking yourself that most important question about who you think will profit more with your money. Them or you? Considering, I'm sure you will be honest with yourself. Why shouldn't you profit from the right answer? And you will be amazed how many times you answer that question correctly concerning many businesses on the stock exchange. I ask again, why shouldn't you profit from them too? Especially if you're a consumer of the businesses' products or their services. Sh** you might as well get them to pay you for being a customer by investing in them. See how we flip this money and keep it moving in a constant flux. After you begin this lifestyle, you will rarely go out and not see the businesses you invest in making you money. You even spend your money differently trying to get value for every dollar you put into circulation.

Confidence breeds success for sure. If you're not confident in what you're doing, it is understandable why you should get out of the market or hire someone else to do your bidding for you. It is an option and it's a better one than stacking money in a bank earning you absolutely nothing!

After doing all the research and sifting through every inch of data I can find on a business that I'm interested in, I then track the price action of the stock -

the highest it's ever been - the lowest it's ever been - comparing it to many time frames - backtesting it for many years on charts and the whole deal. Once I have what I need, I take the trade and wait. You can adopt a style like this on day one with very little thought just the research necessary to know what you're buying and how to use the indicators, charting patterns and reading those candlesticks and moving averages. Isn't that what we do when we buy a car or home? We do the research first so we know who and what we're buying. A walk-through the home or a Test-drive right? Check it out, compare it to other cars like it, and so on. I'm letting you know how I take some trades because success is duplicatable. Like franchises, if you do what they do you will be successful like them, but you'll probably have to act like they act as well. #NoGuarantee

All the moves or strategies I acquire and use I record in my journal to keep me on track and to continue to refer to what's been working so I'm not tempted to get fancy and so should you. How to buy low and sell high, which I believe you already know how to do that. We've been doing it all our lives, just waiting for the price of something to go down so we could benefit on the savings of that product. The difference in the stock market you wait for your price to make more money not to spend it. Also, there is such a thing as a new high as there is a new low price and then a higher high or a lower low depending where the stock is at in its cycle. There are a quite a few variables you learn to keep up with to know the movement of a stock of a company you like.

There's this thing called backtesting where you study the history of the charts of the companies you want to own. You can look up the history of the movement of their stock going back to however old the corporation is. A stock price isn't always an indication of how well or how long a company has or will continue to grow and make a profit. So before putting any money down we log all what we learn in our journals to keep up with the stories of each investment. A crackhead told me to buy low and sell high. He was rich and famous but on crack and he told *me* I had to learn to buy low and sell high. I was like, but you're high! Turns out he knew what he was talking about. You never know where the life lessons are going to come from stay open. #WallStGame

. . .

Buying low and selling high takes some know-how and you need to know how that stock's been moving over the years. So, you don't buy it too high at the top like most participants at the end of a cycle. There's this dude on YouTube who teaches candlesticks and moving averages to his listeners, and he always says most folks buy their shares of stock exuberantly at the top. It's crazy. It's psychological, it must be a lack of patience and knowledge. Be the hunter, not the hunted. Track the stocks for several weeks, even months if necessary. Learn its resistance and support levels throughout its life. Backtest the chart. It will tell you what you need to know about its past movements but not necessarily the full story about its future movements, but it will give you the probability of its future movement.

Learn to think in probabilities, not in knowing. We know nothing. But we probably can make a strong positive assessment about most companies and investments that we research and learn what we need to know to make a profitable decision. If you become a hunter of these markets, this type of mindset allows you the time to study the balance sheet (never be in a hurry to make a move if you're being rushed into a position, you probably shouldn't do it) and the latest story on the company's business and what kind of future growth and profits are they planning and sharing on conference calls. Are they doing buybacks of their own stock or forecasting lower growth, etc? Oh yeah, these folks have conference calls exposing crucial information and you're allowed to listen in. Fundamentals count, but the P/E of a company has nothing to do with the movement of their stock. That's something you must see for yourself on the charts so you can have the confidence in its highest probability of the direction it lives in. Up or down, trend or no trend, volatile or not. Every trader I ever learned anything from that was profitable records their activity in a journal.

So, because I wish nothing but success for you all, I want you to have one too and know the importance of having it and using it. I remember taking some time off from writing in my journal and I'll never do that again. I felt like I was leaving money on the table because I wasn't keeping myself informed about my business. As you gather more chair time in front of the screens, you'll see how your objectives will serve you well. I can't hammer that home enough how knowing your objectives clearly and keeping them in perspective at all times is half your battle to entering CPT's (consistently profitable trades) but you will soon see how they coordinate if you haven't already.   Including your contributions, you will slowly but surely like the tiniest of turtles climb up the back of the big boys and ride to higher profits. Don't let the "greater fools" scare you out of getting your money. I remind you it's your money you're interested in keeping, not anyone else's. Let's stay in our lanes and write all of what you learn in your journals.

INDEXES/ETF

QUICKLY, I'd like to address index funds and the ETFs (exchange-traded funds). I'm sure you've heard of them and if you're new to trading and investing sometimes it's all you hear about. I mean ninety-nine percent of them will always hear if you don't know nothing and don't have time to learn anything to get into index funds. And I say if you're reading this book you know something and if you want to, you can create your own index fund. An Index Fund is nothing more than a basket of stocks grouped together to be sold as one. It's like investing in a team of stocks and you can pick your team. I like to think of my entire portfolio as my professional team. Even my profits I calculate as points instead of dollars. It makes pull backs easier to mentally digest. If your account is down and not out, say, 200.00 points. It's easier to see it down 200.00 points than two hundred dollars. #Psyche

For example, the QQQ ETF is a tech team of stocks, then the most popular are the SPY, SPX, and Vanguard funds, VFINX, VFIAX. Most function as ETFs (exchange-traded funds) some are mutual funds. We players stay away from the mutual's for now. The strategy isn't mutually agreeable to smaller accounts. And that's because mutual funds can have extra charges to your account that you don't want to pay early in the game. Some as high as 10,000.00 dollars is required for a minimum investment. Wait 'til you have so much money you don't want to tell people you have any. Then maybe look into Mutual funds if you're in your senior years.

However, the ETF's we fu** with you can buy a basket of stocks a share or two at a time. It's also a great way to hedge some of your positions in these sectors. Hedging is used in the "real" streets a little differently. It's more of an understanding than a mathematical computation, but it adds up to the same thing. It's basically CYA (cover your assets). If this doesn't pay you, something else will. Hedge your bet when you're betting but I'm asking you for your benefit to Google hedging when you can and get Wall Street's full explanation and the various ways of implementing it into your trading style. #KISS

If the QQQ is at 190.00 dollars, you pay zero commission to enter or exit the trade. That's because in 2019 all major brokerages went to zero commissions to buy or sell a stock they were hitting us up for 4.95 to buy and sell and before that 10.00 and so on and so on. No more for us, it's zero. So, you end up paying the exact amount for one share of QQQ at 190.00 bucks, but you get a basket of stocks and not all the same stocks but usually a well-diversified group of them. Another way to understand it is they select an array of stocks in the sector the ETF is focused on. You can get an ETF on whether or not the sun will come up in the morning. They have almost every thought or sector packaged up in an ETF. You can buy an ETF that selects only companies that women are the CEOs of, for example. Your homework would be to go to your brokerage account and discover and research, what stocks the QQQ and other ETF's are holding and do you want to invest in what they have to offer. How does it compare and move with the other ETF's and especially the SPX index? I use the QQQ and the SPX as market indicators to get a better understanding of the dynamics of the market for the day while I'm trading. Okay, now you're left with the earnings expectation of 10% annually if you buy into this way of investing.

The expectation of other investors and traders who don't have the same objectives as you do for your life will tell you to invest into indexes because it's easy. I listen to advice like guideposts but not actual advice. I returned much more than 10% my first year. Beginner's luck I'm sure because I haven't done it since, but I did it. Just saying live up to your own expectations of you and not others just listen for the data it might be useful. If you decide you want to sit on the bench and make your money do that but make your money. Do the due diligence and put some money to work in these ETF's if they fit your strategy and objectives. Many of the thousandaires do it by sitting on the bench or standing on the sidelines. Sh**, you could be up in the stands in the last row and make money in the stock market. That's what's so great about this industry. You get to make the decisions for your portfolio and decide on the strategy you use to get your money. I don't know if I can trust someone else making decisions for my money more than I trust me. I will listen to all opportunities, but I will make the final decision to buy or sell.

Stock picking does take much more skill and a great deal of due diligence and a gang of Wall Street Smarts, which I know you have because you attracted this book into your life. Only folks with main street, real street game will understand this book and its purpose. "The Others" that's what we'll call 'em "The Others," the ones that would cut you out of the stock market with horrifying headlines and half-truths to continue to scare you into doing only one thing with your hard earned money and that's to spend it. When you hear in the news how well consumer spending is going and creating strength in the market, that's us, me and you, before we became investors. Now we get paid for our spending too. I guess the greedy (market makers) figure every one of us can't or won't be investors. Somebody has to spend to make ROC (return on capital) or the ROI (return on investment) in order for these companies to be profitable. We, the population, have to be spending. So now as investors, we get to contribute (deposit cash) to ourselves. #ThatPart

THE TECH/THE TRADING STATION

I THOUGHT it would be fun to share with you all the tech and equipment that I used to start making trades and investments. I know this will be useful to you as guideposts and not advice. Funny thing is I had to first learn what buttons to press in the software provided by the brokerage firm to make a trade. I had to figure out how the software worked on my new account before ever investing into any new equipment. #Udig

I let you in on this truth because admittedly it was a lil' embarrassing not understanding the software at first. I actually lost a $4,800.00 profit on some OTC "pump and dump" (something else for you to

Google) that my guy who helped me open my account told me to buy. I lost the profit because I didn't know how to dump while they pumped (sell button). At the time I didn't even know what a "pump and dump" was. I didn't know what was happening except there was $4,800.00 on my screen and I didn't know how to get it out of the screen and into my P&L column (profit and loss). By the time I called the brokerage firm to ask how to do it, it was dumped back to a lower price than it was originally bought for. This is something you never forget, and it was my first real lesson of how these markets will do you and that you should know what you're buying and understand how to sell it when you want to. Also, it proved to me there was real money to be made in these markets. I just had to learn how to get it.

So, you see, this was quite a dramatic thing to happen to a new investor it was emotionally disturbing and exciting at the same time. I tell you this to give you the heads up, so you won't have to make any similar mistakes at the beginning. Call your brokerage firm. Take your time getting started. I'll repeat "don't be in a hurry to lose money." So first, get the necessary tutorial on what you need to know to run your software and make money. Be willing to look dumb at first so the market doesn't make you feel dumber later.   This is what I call a PSA (public service announcement) in a book. It has to be a first.

I share because I care about you not letting something like what I did stop you from doing you. "Mistakes will be made but they're not made forever." Bond, James Bond. I couldn't help it. You know that sounds like a title for a Bond film. "Mistakes will be made but they're not made forever" to a theater near you. #LOL

Anyways get over it. I did. Maybe, if you hear it here first, you might not be so quick to make these kinds of mistakes. If you don't know something, ask somebody. Never feel embarrassed about protecting your business. Sometimes when I have to call my brokerage firm for information, I let them know right up front. I say things like. I don't care how stupid my question might sound to you, but I need you to answer it. And they're always super nice to me after they get a good laugh. I have never had an unanswered question by them. We're so blessed these days to have the independence to run your own fund. If you think about it, these are all the employees you don't have to hire. Just pick up the phone and call 'em. #Brokerage

Not knowing and having to learn takes an effort obviously half of America is not interested in putting out. So, I'm out here spreading the word to reignite the interest it might take for main street to make that effort. No, everyone is not cut out for this, but I believe there are more people that are than we know and those are the millions of Americans that I'm writing this book for. It's the knowing and if they don't know or aren't made aware, then there's nothing they can do about it. So, I'm telling.

OKAY! Let's talk equipment. I have to tell you I like to think of myself as "Mission Impossible" private. Well, as much as I can afford to be, you might say. I keep my cellphones in privacy pouches to block unwanted notifications. This is why the journal is absolutely necessary for me. This is me I don't trust the tech and not that I don't trust it, I don't trust the people running it.

They're some tricky people out there and if you've ever seen a coder, coding or even a webmaster which you might be yourself, build a website and they show you how the back end of your website looks you'll know it's above my pay grade and intelligence. Which means I could be violated for my personal data or my tech could be infected by some malware virus at any time and I wouldn't know what's going on. These are part of the *Invisible Intangibles*. The Sh** that could happen.

My journals are handwritten accounts of all the moves in my portfolio from cash balances to the price of the next equity I'm considering investing in and all the notes that I need to consider the buy. Day to day I write. Back up number two is of course the brokerage firm I keep my accounts with, they have everything about me and my accounts in their computers. My books, if I was a gangsta, these are the books you want to get hold of. #Hackers

I digress, tech is just unreliable, the weather is still the ruler of the atmosphere and will put tech in a choke hold on a bad day. Rarely do we hear anyone who prepares you, the retail investor, for such inconveniences or mishaps with the tech or equipment they've chosen to use in their homes. Blackouts, strong winds and floods happen all the time, especially these days. Don't get caught sleeping and if your unit shuts down for the day because of bad weather or some outage on your block. Don't freak out. The stock market will be where you left it once you're back up. Your stocks may not be but remember this too shall pass.

However, when I began to actively trade, I was wise enough to know not to run out and buy some big ass Bloomberg station, though I surely like how they look. I wasn't going to hock anything to look like I knew what I was doing. I was going to wait 'til I actually knew what I was doing. So, what I did was use all the tech I already owned. I had two cellphones (a Samsung Galaxy and a Blackberry) I had an iPad and two MacBooks (laptops) a new one and an old white one. It's an antique now. I still have it in case a museum wants it someday. I had to keep it plugged in for it to work as soon as it disconnected from the power it shuts down. I felt lucky to have these pieces.

I know some of us who've started with less and others with more.

Basically, I'm suggesting the same thing for anyone new to the markets before investing into huge 34-inch screens and a new computer system. See how well you do with what you have. Though I believe many of you who read my books have the Wall Street Smarts to earn more than the four hundred dollars Americans seem to be missing. I wouldn't want to encourage anyone to spend a gang of money upfront on new equipment to look or feel like a real live trader. I want you to know what you're doing and make that decision for yourselves. As I've already mentioned previously everybody isn't cut out for the markets so why put out all that cash before you know you're going to fall in love with this Wall Street Game or at minimum you like having money all the time. You'll know when you're ready to upgrade. I can't tell you and no one else should.

I figure if I share with you what I was working with at the time it will give you all no reasons or excuses to not try. You know the saying "if I can do it, sh** you can do it" it goes something like that. I knew I was good to go when I made enough money to actually buy the equipment I work on now in my office. Which by the way I didn't have either when I started but the extra money I was saving and pulling out of the market (a 1000.00 dividend you might say. That Yang money!) allowed me to move to a bigger house with an office and a view. I think that's a good indication you should upgrade the equipment you're working on when you've made more than enough money to buy an upgrade of your system and even then, you don't have to get fancy or extravagant. You'll see later my next upgrade was a frugal purchase. What I'm trying to convey in this topic is don't wait for it either. Don't wait to get the big screens and machines to get started, you can get started right now saving and making the money for the big screens. Just pull your phone out and maybe grab your laptop and begin and if you only have a cellphone begin slowly. But don't let not having the screens you see other traders posing in front of stop you from getting started. This is what I'm trying to make clear here. It reminds me of when I used to hear new comics say about their stand-up material. They would tell me as soon as they get a tight fifteen minutes of material they're going to get on stage.

You'd hear them say, "I'm just not ready." I used to tell 'em, "You'll never be ready." And they never were. Sushi is never ready and people eat it and sell it to others for money every day. Waiting creates more waiting. So, don't wait to "rob the rich" legally in the stock market when they're just begging you to take their money. #LOL

My next upgrade from the phones and iPad was a frugal purchase which I've mentioned earlier I would even go as far to say it was a cheap purchase. I don't mess around with cheap stuff much but in this case; I didn't understand everything I would need right away, so I was going to buy something I could give away to someone else or just throw away. See, I, we, have to do the due diligence in shopping for one of these bad boys you just don't want to shell out a few grand and buy the wrong computer. I bring that up because in moving too fast in the past I would make a mistake like that. Trading has helped me slow my roll in many ways today.

When I made the leap from my phones, iPad and laptops I ended up with a pre-used dual screens 17 inches desktop computer. It was a Dell mostly. I say that because the monitors weren't Dell. I forget what brand they were, but the keyboard and computer were a Dell. I got it off of Amazon for like $260.00. It was cool to me and I would still use my iPad with it and the extra laptop to make the actual trades. I didn't feel safe pulling the trigger with a pre-owned PC, so I did them on my Apple laptop. I was as professional as I could get for the moment. I knew I would need a faster computer soon, but it was fun seeing my account swell to the point that I could afford a new one. #Goals

Now my knowledge of computers and which speed is good for you is nil. You must do your homework here. I had to get my nephew who's a computer whiz to help me shop and plug in my new system. If you don't have a nephew like mines, a brilliant young man, you'll have to rely on the professionals who sell them. There are plenty of traders online that also offer detailed assistance on finding you an affordable and competent computer system. I have a super-duper fast desktop computer now. I got it at Best Buy with three 34-inch monitors and a 50-inch that sits on its own stand for TV viewing and the ticker scroll.

I have a wireless and a wire keyboard with a wireless mouse. Oh yeah, and it's a HP. I also have a travel unit. It's a Dell laptop (www.Dell.com) fixed with two monitors, wireless keyboard and mouse with carrying cases for all the pieces. That's it. I'm sure you'll be able to get what you want once you start saving and making some of that "Yang money." #Dividends

K.I.S.S.
KEEP IT SIMPLE STRATEGIES

EVERY ONCE IN A WHILE, you'll hear on the street a gender battle about who makes a better trader a man or a woman? First of all, it's a dumb ass question or comparison because women weren't encouraged to get involved in this game either. It was always thought of as a man's game, like every other game in this country. Discrimination is a killer of much talent. But these ladies were left out too and I'm specifically talking about the highly elite educated woman. So, you know the powers to be didn't care about the other ninety-nine percent of women in these real streets or on main street. Who's trying to pull them up? Answer: Nobody except me now, I guess, I hope so. What I mean is I hope that my books have helped as many women as men. I have daughters and I have encouraged them both to get into this game and they have yet to do it, but I believe one day they will. I have to look out for 'em for now, but when and if it ever resonates with them to become investors, I'll be their greatest supporter. I share this with you because if you think ninety-nine percent of Americans with less than four-hundred dollars are only made up of men, you're truly mistaken. I know so many women that aren't up on this game that I think would be great at it and I tell 'em every chance I get. Women should be encouraged to come up just like the men in these markets. It's my bias opinion to say I believe that a huge number of women would be better traders than most men who think they're smarter than everyone else.

So, I hope women are reading this book and understand the purpose of knowing the Wall Street Game and go onto do well for themselves. Go on and get that money too. My books are for all humans with the savvy to take over the direction of their financial future. Let's go ahead now and share some simple strategies I've picked up and where I picked them up so you can reference the material yourself. These little tidbits of knowledge can apply to your trading immediately. Depending on how fast you read and on the sense of urgency to learn and know what you're doing. Some of my success is simply "Wall Street Smarts" intuitive as I have a feeling everyone reading my books has this same tool in their arsenal of behavior. Most real down-to-earth people have this intuitiveness to recognize and then acknowledge bullsh** when they hear it. So, beginning with most news outlets and publications, it's clear to me and I am fully aware at all times they are in favor of the fat cats and not me or you. I take that to heart and move only according to my objectives and financial goals. So, yes, you will hear it again because it's half my strategy as a lil' turtle riding on the back of the huge ones. #WayoftheTurtle

Before Monday even gets here and that bell rings, remember there is no real bell in the market. It means absolutely nothing about how well your stocks are going to do that day. So, before it even rings on every Monday on the weekends I'm plotting my probabilities of what to buy or sell. Sell on strength and buy on weakness. Reduce cost basis whenever I can allocate funds to do so. If you learn to just do those things, you'll be doing good. Knowing my objectives and what I want to accomplish today and overall as an investor is absolute. What do I need? What do you need? Let's start with that "Yang" money; the extra thousand dollars a month by creating your on UBI (universal basic income).

Now, what you must understand, you may not always make a thousand dollars every month (early stages) but you'll have access to a thousand or more every month. And that's what it's all about having money and not always making money, you just have to make it, to have it, so if you can learn to marry the two together you can stay paid. What I mean is this, you're starting with an amount as low as fifteen-hundred dollars and you have to keep that in perspective in these early stages. Those of you who can start with 10K or 15K or more, super, but I don't want to discourage anyone from growing whatever amount of money they have to start with.

This is the purpose of my books to get every amount in the market. If I waited to have 10K or 15K to start trading I wouldn't have that kind of money now. I built my account to those amounts and more and it's my belief millions of Americans can do it too and eliminate this not having four hundred extra dollars for anything they want. However, you raise the money to start off with doesn't matter (Well if you steal it, that's not good. Jus' joking, not). What matters is that you began a lifetime of contributing to your own ATM balance and investment capital. I haven't read any books that encourage Americans that are making everyday wages how to invest or trade their everyday wage money. Some of you I swear will do better than me financially because you have consistent wages, whereas, my lifestyle is very inconsistent. I have to wait on acting, comedy or writing jobs.

If you work for UPS, FedEx or even Amazon or any of these millions of gig paying jobs, who offer IRA's which is good and bad but makes no difference that shouldn't stop you from opening your own personal account to make more money, you're missing out on increasing that income on your own. Forget what your job is doing. That money you save with your job's IRA will hopefully be there when you exit that job but it's not liquid now so you shouldn't concern yourself with it. When you leave that job, you can roll it over to your personal fund you now have.

With your own account you may start becoming so financially endowed you won't have to go into work as often as used to. Sometimes when you see yourself compounding interest receiving dividends and increasing your own money, it opens up a myriad of possibilities to that person. Like quitting that job and starting something new on your own. At our incomes, we'll always have to replace our income if we quit or got laid off to feed the beast - our accounts. You'll be feeding the beast, contributing to yourself, paying yourself until you don't have to. It beats the alternative "broke-ness" forever. So, one of your main objectives is to have control over how much you poke at the beast. You never want to be all in. That's a sure recipe for losing money. Always remember nothing is out, it's just down. All winning trades look like losers along the way to sometimes get rid of the weak and the nonbelievers of the particular companies stock you invested into. Or some other invisible intangible we don't know about. Poking the beast would be always taking from it before adding to it. More with-draw of money, than deposits. Capital allocation and risk management is crucial. It's what keeps the trader, the investor with liquid cash. Learn how not to feel the need to be all in when it means wiping out your account balance. Never wipe it out and I do mean never, ever, ever. Just wait 'til you consider what you're about to do, which is leave yourself broke without liquid cash to spend in any way you may see fit. From the lyrics of the good prophet LL Cool J, "Don't do it dog!"

That's your money and you'll have to be responsible for it now. It will be up to you to manage the positions you're holding the stocks, while you're learning and studying about rotation and market cycles and the dynamics of the market and if any stories have changed concerning the company's stock that you own. Oh yeah, anyone tell you once you bought a stock, you're actually an owner of that business. If you own one share of Microsoft, that's how much of that company you're now the owner of.

You built this account and so it's on you how you spend from it. Always keep some of the balance in cash. With fifteen hundred dollars to start with, a third of that I kept in cash, which would be five hundred dollars. Then I waited long enough to profit from my buys, sold out of them, and did it again and again while contributing each week more dollars to allocate when necessary. So now think about it, no matter what happens with the thousand you have decided to put on some reliable stocks. You'll always have five hundred dollars extra liquid for whatever you want that month. As long as you don't find a reason to spend it as you're adding to your contributions, that balance and third will get bigger and bigger with time. Time is your best friend. It won't be long until you'll realize the swelling of your account caused by compound interest and dividends alone, where in no time at all, your cash balance will be at an amount that looks good to you. Congratulations, you're the next Thousandaire!

DELAYED GRATIFICATION

DELAYED GRATIFICATION these are the two biggest words in this book for one reason without it you will fail. In short, if the money you're investing with is a small amount like the fifteen hundred dollars I began with or less you should know if you need to use that money to pay bills or to make you money. The advantages I have learned with starting out with a small account and with no real experience trading in these volatile markets is that I too was made to be afraid of it. As you find a strategy for what kind of trading you'd like to do, I like to suggest that it's much easier being an investor (a contrarian) than it is being a day trader not that you can't or shouldn't or won't take a day trade or swing trade once you get the hang of trading. From my experience it's better to learn the *Way of the Turtle* and it's what I suggest to my family, friends and clients. It's more profitable being a contrarian trader than a barbarian one (day trader). Peter Lynch, Warren Buffett, Joel Greenblatt, these are three of the top investors in the world - all contrarian - Value Investors.

Opening a smaller account has its advantages. It's possible and doable. It's not a far fetch goal for most of the population to raise five or fifteen hundred dollars to begin his or her investment portfolios. The social environment just makes you feel like it's impossible because it's been impossible for them collectively. And everything in our society is about "ballin'."

Now I know you're going to say, "Hey Mr. Spencer, you've been telling us that the polls have been saying that no one in America has an extra four hundred dollars to their name for anything extra." And you would be right, they don't, but most have four hundred dollars extra to make more money. They may or may not have to decide which bill not to pay this month or move some things around on the old budget. You may not have four hundred extra dollars to spend in an emergency, but if you had one 911, somebody wouldn't be getting paid this month, would they? Those bill collectors would have to wait by no other choice. So again, the stats say the average American household doesn't have the money to spend, but I believe they could find it. If they knew how and believed, they can make more money with it. It's just "Wall Street Smarts" (makes sense).

Turning a little money into a bunch of it, that's what this and all my books are about. I'm not catering to the rich folks who have it. I'm employing the least of us who would be left out of making more money because we've been told or made to believe we're not rich enough to get into it. I too had to get with the delayed gratification thing at the beginning (emotional discipline). It's something we have to wrap our heads around. I need my money now, brotha' is what I usually hear from Americans afraid to get started.

Most folks think to themselves I can't do that investing business because it takes too long to get paid, while all along they're spending every dime of their capital (earnings) they could use to invest with on everyday needs. Some of those needs are wants and that money could be reallocated towards investing. Instead, it's spent to never be seen again, to never benefit them in any way in the future. We, you, have to now go out and bring home more money from a job or somewhere but it's never ending. The rent, mortgage and car note have to be paid.

One of my closest actor friends came to me with five hundred dollars to start with. At first I told 'em he was crazy but with his understanding of delayed gratification and contributing to himself each week sometimes once a month he built his account up in less than three years to have over ten grand extra to his name and personal balance sheet. Before you shoot this timeframe down, ask yourself in the last few years how much extra cash do you have? And I do mean extra. Time passes fast when you're making money. There's never enough of it. And when you're not making any money, you seem to have all the time in the world. It moves much slower.

.   .   .

Beginning with a small account like I've described allows for a gang of mistakes and it forces you to become disciplined. Because you respect the game now and your bottom line. The discipline it takes to trade a smaller account will mold you into a disciplined investor which is what you want to be. It'll give you what you need to know to manage millions one day if that's in the cards for you. What one does with little, one can do with much. Now the big shots may say about my actor friend that ten thousand extra bucks in three years is nothing. Because he's not ballin' at all, but my friend would say he wouldn't care what they had to say because the objectives he's meeting are his own. He's happy he knows what makes him feel good. He doesn't need millions. Yet. He knows how to keep his life and money in perspective. He knew he wasn't becoming a millionaire with his account. He actually used to be one. But now, right now, today at all times he has over four hundred dollars extra and much more for anything he wants. Before the pandemic, dude was traveling all over the world, him and his lady. I guess he's doing fine, better than most of Americans. Right? At least according to the media that say we're all broke. I was glad I could be a part of helping him do that.

. . .

Myself, I like to keep at least ten grand handy as a cash balance for whatever I might want or need. When I get below that I get concerned and I make a way to get my money higher. With an extra twenty or thirty thousand dollars to spend on any given day makes me feel quite comfortable for the most part. More is good and I anticipate more every day because I can. Because I got started when I did with what I had. The kicker is with a higher cash balance on hand. It allows you to be on point to swoop up all of the highest of probability stocks you've been hunting down to make you even more money. It's what I like to do, which is a simple strategy to stay a CPT (consistent profitable trader). The more profits you make, the higher cash balance you can hold on to throughout your investment career. You'll hear many traders blabbing in the "game" about being all in the market and that you should be all in too. Suggesting that you don't leave any cash on the side because that's cash that's not making you any money. Yet. I like the word yet, because if you do the due diligence, researching these businesses and understanding the movements of their stocks. Having a cash balance at all times and knowing stocks like you will after doing the due diligence. You will be able to recognize the pattern of how to buy low or lower and sell high or higher. It gets simple. It really does, though. The market attempts to complicate it with all its fancy words and math. But you, we can take advantage of that. It's called an edge. Instead of doing what most participants do, which is the opposite - buying high and selling low (just understanding that small bit of game you should be determined to not do what they do).

Too many of us get caught up in it until we learn to stop it. Always take small positions at first, 2 or 3 shares even, that way if the stock moves in an unfavorable direction because we got something wrong, we can buy it lower and recoup any downward action of the stock. If it goes higher, you get paid anyway. It's actually better that it went down further because when it zags back to the "mean" you'll make a bigger profit than you originally believed you would when you took the trade. Too many new investors jump in the stock market without understanding delayed gratification and blow their accounts out in weeks. You have to allow your investment to grow. You plant a seed. You don't go back in two minutes and see if the flower has grown. Only in the stock market do participants do that. #DayTrading

---

You, we, wait for it.

In the stock market, traders sit in front of their screens for the trading session all day long just waiting for that very thing to happen. It can be frustrating and hard on the emotions. If you have the huevos, go ahead but if you're like me and just want to have more money "value investing" is the way to go. However, many of the traders I speak of are equipped with certain knowledge and insider info most of us aren't privy to either.

Somehow once you get in the habit of living the investment life, days, weeks, and years move rather quickly all of sudden delaying gratification is second nature. Because you now have the experience and knowledge to know it makes you money. Then you take that money and put it on a more reliable trade or investment. One that you have learned is now overwhelming in your favor to profit from. Because you know it. Because you did your due diligence and it's been in your journal waiting for you to take advantage of it. This way you'll never really be affected by a loss. You'll always keep an inventory of stocks you would buy in your journal to replace winners you have sold out of for a large profit or a small loss. That's how we do it. Losses are mucho pacquito (small) that way we never have to take a loss we can't make up.

This is some of the Wall Street Game that will become natural for you over the years. With this kind of understanding and perception of trading and investing, you won't have to make a big thing out of losing money. You'll be down, but not out. If the color red fu**s with you, learn to get over it quickly because it's really a distress signal that opportunity is around the corner to make more money.

· · ·

You will hear much talk and noise from the market to scare you out of every position you own every day... all the fu***** time. That's another consistent thing you can count on in the market is that the noise makers will continue to scare people out of their money. I think it's rude but obviously to keep the market going up and down but always up in the long term it's necessary to get rid of some uncommitted folks. But if you can prevent this from happening to you. You'll turn losers into winners throughout your investing lifestyle and become a CPT yourself. #Experience

A note here, you should know the stories are true it is possible your stock is the stock that shot up to new highs today, maybe even in the profit zone you were expecting. Yes, you should know even at the beginning your stock can go up rather quickly. Heads up though, you shouldn't be betting on your stock zooming up to your profit zone every day. Instead, you should know and believe it eventually will because of your chosen edge and strategy and the rules you've made for yourself to follow. You're the referee and the player. Tell me that isn't a win-win situation? As long as no one catches on, you can win a lot of games being both. #HighestProbabilty

When you are finally armed with certain knowledge, you could buy a stock that goes up quickly on any given day to give you a profit. It can happen in a heartbeat and when it happens for the first time, it can make your heart skip a beat. *Trading in the Zone* by Mark Douglas taught many retail investors how to trade like the big boys - the institutions. And a quote you'll hear most of his students quote him on is that "Anything can happen. You don't need to know what is going to happen next in order to make money." People who knew 'em loved this teacher and I suggest you get his book and listen to his YouTube interviews. I think main street loved Mark too. You should enjoy Mark. He was a quirky, funny dude and a really nice guy.

I think this fast action that can happen in the stock market is what attracts so many gamblers to the market, but those with Wall Street Game know better than to gamble. #Edge

· · ·

If you're investing and you made a trade that zoomed up for a huge profit in a day or a week... go ahead and take it, take the money. That's what we got in this for. Don't be afraid to take the money. What I want understood with delayed gratification, don't expect that to happen every day on every stock pick you have chosen. After you've sold out of a position for a profit, open a new trade you've already had your eye on. And keep the one you sold out of for a profit in your journal, and if you ever see it being pushed back down below where you know you can take the trade again for a profit then do it. That's what we do, we keep sticking it to it as long as it rides upwards. Buying low and selling high.

You will hear a strategy constantly used by other traders, not investors to describe what I'm sharing with you as buying a dip or a drawdown and then expect the stock to go up even higher. No, no, that's not what I've written here. There may be no overwhelming profit to be made in buying on a dip and there's nothing to say it would go higher after it dipped. It might go lower. Learning to read charts and candlesticks can help you with making those decisions.

. . .

We're looking for that stock price to be distressed again - the Bat-Signal! We follow it right back to the price where we might have originally found it or close enough. That would be the first distress signal that a stock you used to own has fallen back where you bought it from in the first place. If it goes lower cool, we'll take that. Sometimes you'll find the entire sector in distress and there you go. There's money to be made.

You want that stock price pushed all the way back down to the price you bought it for before you made a profit on it. Wash and repeat that. Once you learn its movements, it can turn into an automatic money maker for you every time. As long as the company we're talking about is a growing profitable business to remain in business for years to come at least for the next ten or twenty years. Enough time to earn the profits you're seeking. What's this play coach? It's a most simplistic strategy. It also informs the new investor how your investment just became a trade. A trade that if your information is right about the long-standing growth of this company, you can take over and over on its continued ride upwards. *Confusion De Confusiones* - get this book and get back with me. The "scare" has been a part of these markets since the 1600's. This most simplistic strategy has been played for centuries and is the easiest of them all.

Now, of course, if it's that easy why isn't everyone doing it? The psychological effect the market has on its participants is above my pay grade, but I study and read about it all of the time to get an understanding of it. Buying low and selling high is harder for some I think because buying low is equated with cheap and buying high somehow is equated with making money "the trend" a trending pattern. Well, you can go with that or you can believe me (game recognize game) and make profitable returns on your investments.

If you were rich already, you could buy the entire stock market and take money out every day. It's what all the big "players" do and what the rest of us dream of doing as soon as we can. Understand if we're in the game we have a better chance of that happening than not. But if you're not in the game, there's no chance of that at all. Being in the game creates opportunities. Not only are we doing well for now (meeting our objectives) but our future could attract a great deal of money to us because we think of our growing assets all the time now. Like attracts like. And because of that subconsciously we'll attract more money to us. Not for the love of money, but for the independence of having money.

You now have a place to park a huge amount of money (expected and unexpected) that you never had before. Once your belief system picks up on what I'm writing about, you'll say to yourself, "Oh yeah, I do. I could park helluva cash here and turn it into more cash." There are many investment tools out there to buy once you're super rich but if you're just rich or a thousandaire, the stock market is how we keep the money liquid and making profitable returns. #Alchemist

Now we just created our own UBI (universal basic income) and that thousand-dollar dividend is now a thing of the past. You have that kind of money available to you at all times now. #YangMoney

. . .

You'll be the only one in the room, break room, board room, dining room with more than a thousand dollars on hand immediately. You'll be the only one of your peers that has the extra cash that so many are still without. There's so much game to share with you about these markets that I have learned in my short time as a CPT (consistent profitable trader). I don't know if I'll ever be able to write it all down for you all and it keeps evolving every year. I had so much more I wanted to share with you in this book, but I purposely thought I should keep my books short because I know this kind of information is best in small bites. I told you guys at the beginning I wasn't some rich dude over in some high rise making sh** up in books to protect my millions.

If you're the right candidate for my first two books (*Wall Street Smarts* and *Turning Losers into Winners In The Stock Market*) and of course the one you're reading now number three; if you have applied and studied the material in all three books, you might have learned enough to wean yourself off of me and start to take on more astute and well-mannered authors with more expertise in the markets than I. If you can stick with me over the years though, I will continue to give you what I learn with no cut on it. Straight, no chaser. And I'm confident you have moved past not having money all of the time because now you have learned how to accumulate wealth. Stack racks! #CashBalance

One... I'm putting one up in the air for My Thousandaires! I'm out for now. #Micdrop

THE END

PLEASE LEAVE A REVIEW!

If you have enjoyed getting up on the game, I would be ever so grateful if you could spread the word.

With being a new author, reviews help me gain visibility and they can bring my books to the attention of other potential thousandaires who wish to improve their financial situations.

Leaving a review on Amazon helps others find this book more easily. To leave a review, please click below. Thank you in advance. #PayItForward

THOUSANDAIRE MOVEMENT

Thank you for purchasing this book and investing your time in reading it. It really means a lot to me. If you've enjoyed Wall Street Smarts, go ahead and join the Thousandaire Movement for updates, announcements and giveaways.

It's completely free to sign up and you will never be spammed by me. You can opt out easily at any time.

Go to www.wallstsmarts.com and join Thousandaire Movement by subscribing.

MORE BOOKS FROM YUL SPENCER

Wall Street Smarts

Turning Losers Into Winners In The Stock Market

K.I.S.S. Keep It Simple Stock Market

For More Information
www.wallstsmarts.com

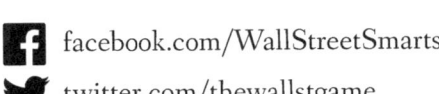 facebook.com/WallStreetSmarts
twitter.com/thewallstgame
instagram.com/wallstsmarts

WEBSITES

StockCharts

Investors Hub

TradingView

Seeking Alpha

Market Watch

Small Cap Power

FinViz (stock screener)

Guru Focus

The Fly

Tiingo

Earnings Cast Calls

SOCIAL MEDIA

StockTwits

FinTwit (Twitter)

Instagram

Reddit

Linkedin

Facebook

BOOKS

- Stock Trader's Almanac by Jeffrey A. Hirsch
- A Complete Guide to Volume Price Analysis by Anna Coulling
- Way of the Turtle by Curtis M. Faith
- Market Cycles by Howard Marks
- 100 Best Stocks to Buy in "(current year)" by Peter Sander and Scott Bobo
- Winning the Mental Game on Wall Street by John Magee
- What Works on Wall Street by Jim O'Shaughnessy
- Market Mind Games by Denise Shull
- Big Mistakes by Michael Batnick
- The New Market Wizards by Jack D. Schwager

- Your Money Your Brain by Jason Zweig
- The Little Book that Still Beats the Market by Joel Greenblatt
- An extra author for the list who writes really easy to understand stock market books is Matthew R. Kratter. Check him out on Amazon.

ABOUT THE AUTHOR

European born actor, **YUL SPENCER,** is a multi-talented performer whose career encompasses television, film, animation, theater, and standup comedy. As a comic, he went by the name of Spencer, toured nationally and has appeared on HBO, Comedy Central and eight seasons on BET's Comic-View. He has acted in hit TV shows like *The Shield and* Malcolm & Eddie, numerous films including *Two Can Play That Game* with Vivica A. Fox and various national commercials.

Yul was inspired for several reasons to write a series of books on the stock market, because many of his colleagues at his age had no "real" money. He was among comedians and actors living a high life because of who they are in the Hollywood industry, but none of them, including himself, had liquid cash or money they had saved. He thought what good is it to be a star at anything and not have access to a minimum of thousands of fu** you dollars.

After contemplating this lifestyle, he wanted to take back control of his finances. Yul wanted to determine how and when money came to him. So, he studied the market for the last ten years and read tons of books and wondered why more regular everyday people aren't investing. Well, what he found out, is that many of the trading books, make things way too complicated and confusing. They're discouraging to the average American. He wanted to write a series of books that offered more encouragement and simplified the way of profiting on the stock market. He felt, if he can do this, anyone can. Though, Yul was born in Europe, he was raised in Oakland, CA. Having been raised in Oakland, Yul has a lot of Street-Smarts, and he has applied his Street-Smarts and Comedy to the Stock Market, because the Stock Market has never been this funny.

These books were written "In response to America's $400.00 Financial crisis." Everyone should have at the very least $400.00 available to them at all times. At his core, Yul believes Americans can put an end to "brokeness" that plagues most citizens. He feels it's time for us all to come up and not let an unexpected $400.00 bill throw us into disarray.

FULL DISCLAIMER

While the author has used his best efforts in preparing this book, he makes no representations or warranties with respect to the accuracy or completeness of the contents of this book and specifically disclaims any implied warranties or merchantability or fitness for a particular purpose. The advice and strategies contained herein may not be suitable for your situation.

You should consult with a legal, financial, tax professional where appropriate. Neither the publisher nor the author shall be liable for any loss of profit or any other commercial damages, including but not limited to special, incidental, consequential, or other damages.

This book is for educational, informational and entertainment purposes only. The views expressed are those of the author alone and should not be taken as expert instruction or commands. The reader is responsible for his or her own actions.

Adherence to all applicable laws and regulations, including international, federal, state, and local laws, is the sole responsibility of the purchaser or reader.

Neither the author nor the publisher assumes any responsibility or liability whatsoever on the behalf of the purchaser or reader of these materials.

Any perceived slight of any individual or organization is purely unintentional.

Past performance is not necessarily indicative of future performance.

Forex, futures, stock and options trading is not appropriate for everyone.

There is a substantial risk of loss associated with trading these markets. Losses can and will occur.

No system or methodology has ever been developed that can guarantee profits of ensure freedom from losses. Nor will it likely ever be.

No representation or implication is being made that using the methodologies or systems or the information contained within this book will generated profits or ensure freedom from losses.

The information contained in this book is for educational, informational and entertainment purposes only and should NOT be taken as investment advice. Examples presented here are not solicitations to buy or sell. The author, publisher, and all affiliates assume no responsibility for your trading results.

THERE IS HIGH RISK IN TRADING!